FIRST EDITION

THE
WISDOM OF
JESUS CHRIST;
ANSWERS

A Christian's Nation Way to Victory

MOFAO N. PHOKA

WESTBOW
PRESS®
A DIVISION OF THOMAS NELSON
& ZONDERVAN

WestBow Press books may be ordered through booksellers or by contacting:

WestBow Press
A Division of Thomas Nelson & Zondervan
1663 Liberty Drive
Bloomington, IN 47403
www.westbowpress.com
844-714-3454

Scripture taken from the King James Version of the Bible.

ISBN: 978-1-6642-4045-2 (sc)
ISBN: 978-1-6642-4044-5 (e)

Print information available on the last page.

WestBow Press rev. date: 07/22/2021

CONTENTS

PREFACE

This book is a special wisdom to Christians. I wrote it under the influence of the gift of revelation by the Holy Spirit. I believe this little book will change your life and make you to face the enemy differently and learn about the wisdom used by our King Lord Jesus during His fight against the devil. Jesus answered the demonic attacks through various ways which includes Scriptural knowledge.

The book tells us on how to defeat the devil through knowledge of scriptures like Jesus Christ did. We learn how important is Submission, how to respond to temptations, and how to scripturally persist in spiritual war. The book also helps us to desire the gift of discernment as it helps in revelation during spiritual wars. Furthermore, Jesus the Christ defeated Satan through parable, nothing, prophetic, evident, rebuking, unquestionable, worship, question by question and factual wisdom.

As Christians following Jesus Christ, we have to follow our Master in all ways and copy exactly the wisdom He used in defeating the devil and his angels. In the next series of the Wisdom books, the various wisdom types shall be explained, especially on how to tap and grow in this wisdom in order to topple down Satan for eternity and become prosperous as the Jesus Nation.

Unless otherwise specified, the bible codes are quoted from King James Version Bible. The book of Luke was used because it is believed to be the orderly account of events.

I hope this book will transform you and you shall look at things differently in the Name of Jesus Christ! **Amen!**

Mofao N. Phoka

DEDICATION

This book is dedicated to Jehovah, Major 1 as the prophet who taught me powerful revelations, my Lesotho ECG Pastor's especially Apostle Wyson Bottoman (National Pastor Lesotho), ECG Mafeteng cell branch Pastor Jimmy Rodgers, Apostle Sayo Mwanyongo family and Pastor Chimwemwe Mkandawire as they taught and revealed mysteries and showed various wisdom chronicles. I will extend my gratitude to my fellow Levite Mr. Seabata Joseph Mongali, my beautiful wife Mrs 'Maphoka Phoka and my children for supporting me in this book writing. They kept encouraging me all the time convening the revelation from the wisdom of Jesus Christ. A special thank-you to all Mafeteng ECG cell Branch Members (2018) for all what they taught me, you made me to write this book. Above all things, I pass my happiness to my parents who are no longer alive for raising me in the Word of God.

CHAPTER ONE

Scriptural Knowledge Wisdom

1. Scriptural Wisdom

Wisdom can be defined as a state of understanding, knowledge, sense, insight, perception, Astuteness, intelligence or acumen which makes the human being or the organism to survive any attack or to gain any good substance to proceed in life smoothly.

Scriptural Wisdom is the high level of wisdom which is supernatural and it straight from God, meaning the Word is God which is God Himself ;- John 1:1

One of deep master key wisdom to all wisdoms and success in anything is to prophetically comprehend the scriptural meaning and knowledge of wisdom of submission, the below paragraph explains the submission.

1.1 Submission Power

We learn a lot as Christians from Jesus Christ, many Christians do not understand the power of submission and what submission can do for one's spiritual life. Jesus is Lord, however Jesus submitted to John and immediately the ministry of Jesus commenced. This means the moment

Christians submit to their spiritual parents their ministry is released immediately and Holy Spirit led and took over regardless of their power and strength.

Matthew 3:14
"But John forbad him, saying, I have need to be baptized of thee, and comest thou to me?"

John did not understand the reason why Jesus came to him. John the Baptist, partially new that Jesus is coming and he could not loose Jesus rope or string of His shoe. Let's read below and realize the power and the wisdom of Jesus Christ while answering the question.

Matthew3:15
"And Jesus answering said unto him, suffer it to be so now: for thus it becometh us to fulfill all righteousness. Then he suffered him".

From the Scripture above, we see Jesus explaining that submission action is the righteousness step all the time. This explain to us the Jesus lived for what is right not of what the flesh and the world believe in. Jesus did not speak of his Power and strength but he did the right thing. God always desire to see his children taking and doing anything rightly to please Him not the world. We also see the Power of the agreement between the two men of God. Though John was surprised, they both agreed. That is, in any submission a Christian take, he or she should agree first with the person he or she is submitting to, otherwise it not righteous.

Moreover, we see John sacrificing when he baptizes Jesus, though Jesus was very senior in Spirit.We learn that, even if someone is senior in Spirit, if God sent him to submit to you, we need to agree and do the righteous activity as described by Jesus to John. The activity of submission must be done "now" and with agreement so that in Heaven it can be known by Holy Spirit.

1.2 Temptations

We realized that after Jesus Christ baptism, the Holy Spirit took over and lead Jesus in wilderness too fast for forty days (40 days) and Satan tempted him. Most Christians after the Holy Spirit take over, Satan tempt them and many fell because of lack of solid foundation. From the Scripture, we will realize that Satan know scripture's and uses it to deceive people, he came with a Word of God, He knows daughters and Sons of God can feel into trap.

Matthew 4:3
"And when the tempter came to him, he said, If thou be the Son of God, command that these stones be made bread".

Be very careful here, the bible records Satan as a tempter, meaning he is good in tempting. Let meshow you where Satan quoted when he attacks Jesus Christ mind set and Spirit.

Deuteronomy 8:3
"And he humbled thee, and suffered thee to hunger, and fed thee with manna, which thou knewest not, neither did thy fathers know; that he might make thee know that man doth not live by bread only, but by every word that proceedeth out of the mouth of the LORD doth man live".

If you look in details, Satan quoted exactly what God said in Deuteronomy 8:3 and attacked Jesus with the word of God. This is the same as demons attacked people in their mindset. Satan fights you with what he knew you like and you know very well. Also, we realize that Satan commands as to make you to be clumsy and if you act abruptly, you will lose it and fall into a trap.Let's see the wisdom of Jesus Christ answer against the devil.

Mathew 4:4
"But he answered and said, It is written, Man shall not live by bread alone, but by every word that proceedeth out of the mouth of God"

The Wisdom of Jesus answer was based on knowledge of the Word of God, meaning Jesus knew the Word, thus knowing the attack of the enemy and He won the battle because of the Word of knowledge. Many Christians follow Jesus but do not know the Word of God and the devil take advantage and attack such Christians. We learn that every attacking answer to devil is in the Word of God. We also learn that man can leave by the Word of God not food as many believe that without food they can die.

Through fasting, we invite the enemy to the battlefield and when you pray while fasting, you shall defeat enemies. There is Power in fasting. You see, when you fast it's like you set the match and enter in a ring with the devil with the Word of God. The devil is meant to trick you with what you know. You need to know exactly the Word of God to win the fight.

Jesus was tempted by some questions found in the bible from the old covenant. This days, when you study the old testament and the new testament, most things has changed and amongst things is; many people hold themselves on the law of Torah and they have forgotten that Jesus change most of the laws. Jesus was attacked through the old ways of Prophet Moses and much contempt him based on such issues. Even you, majority of the Old Testament believers will tempt you just as Jesus was tempted. Below is how Jesus was tempted;

Luke 20:33
"Therefore in the resurrection whose wife of them is she? for seven had her to wife."

If you read at this verse, the Pharisees were challenging Jesus on Moses law, especially the law which rebuke fornication, observe how Jesus answered the people;

Luke 20:34-36

"And Jesus answering said unto them, The children of this world marry, and are given in marriage: Luke 20:35 But they which shall be accounted worthy to obtain that world, and the resurrection from the dead, neither marry, nor are given in marriage: Luke20:36 Neither can they die any more: for they are equal unto the angels; and are the children of God, being the children of the resurrection.".

The wisdom of Jesus Christ answer of this verse above is extremely deep, but it determines the marriage we have with God through Jesus Christ our Lord. It simply explains that there is marriage with God through Him. Love and intimacies are abundant to those who are born again and are with God, meaning, when people ask you about your God or attacking your faith, tell them that, God is a provider of everything for you; the old ways you lived are gone. It should be clear that the spirit of setbacks and the spirit of mindset stagnation or of not being forgetful are attacked by this wisdom. This wisdom attacks the sticky sins in your mind and cleanse you mind. You are now a new creature with God. You will win most of demons if you have the wisdom and you know that your father's name is Jehova-Jireh. I like this verse during counseling of those who new accepted Jesus Christ as their Lord and SAVIOUR.

1.3 The devil persistence

Based on the last chapter, we know that Jesus was attacked by devil. We realize that, the devil will ensure that you know the Word of God through various attacks. That is, you need to know the Word of God fully and use it well to fight the devil. Below is the question asked to Jesus by Devil during the spiritual war. See scripture below,

Mathew 4:6

"And saith unto him, If thou be the Son of God, cast thyself down: for it is written, He shall give his

angels charge concerning thee: and in their hands they shall bear thee up, lest at any time thou dash thy foot against a stone".

As usual, Satan used the Word of God to attack Jesus. Let me show you where devil quoted the scripture he attacked Jesus with.

Psalms (91:11-12)
"For he shall give his angels charge over thee, to keep thee in all thy ways. They shall bear thee up in their hands, lest thou dash thy foot against a stone".

As you read the above scripture and realized how devil can be persistent knocking in your knowledge of Word, you need to know the Word of God fully. Little knowledge of the Word of God is extremely dangerous since Satan can attacked you based on little knowledge~ little faith. See the Wisdom of Jesus Christ answer.

Matthew 4:7
"Jesus said unto him, It is written again, Thou shalt not tempt the Lord thy God".

I will keep emphasizing that, Jesus keeps saying it is written that in his reference replies. This means, Jesus was reading the Word of God from those who came before Him as you see that Jesus was always coding from the book of Deuteronomy. Let me show you again where Jesus coded.

Deuteronomy (6:16)
"Ye shall not tempt the LORD your God, as ye tempted him in Massah".

We deeply see that Satan tempt you while you are at Holy place or church (City) because Angels of God are there to give you something, and the moment you obey Satan, you lose your miracle. Many Christians get tempted in the middle of the church service while about to receive miracles from God Angels. Devil does not want you to concentrate on

God.Jesus clearly depicts that, what God said does not change and he is God of His promise and covenant.

As Christians', it is clear when people of this world start to realizing more about your work, and of what God is doing in your life, they will asked you several questions to tempt you in the knowledge of the word of God. You will find that it is easy to reply them with what they know best, for example, it is easy for the farmer to understand when you say Jesus is the tree of life, just learn the scripture below and follow.

Luke 10:25
"And, behold, a certain lawyer stood up, and tempted him, saying, Master, what shall I do to inherit eternal life?"

This version of the bible use the word "tempt", and you must know that God test while devil tempt, meaning Jesus was asked by evil spirit through the law student who is believed to be studying Torah, but asking to see if Jesus know his scriptures. Study the scripture below and see how Jesus answered the question above;

Luke 26, 28
"He said unto him, What is written in the law? how readest thou?... Luke10:28 And he said unto him, Thou hast answered right: this do, and thou shalt live."

Jesus simply said to the law student that, he should follow and live accordingly to Ten Commandments he has studied and he shall inherit the eternal life, especially the commandment of "love". In life, people who know the Word of God can tempt you. When people who think they know the Word tempt you, answer them accordingly to the degree of their knowledge (gnosis) of the word of God; they turn to understand you fully and comprehensively if you do so. This wisdom of replying people in accordance to their knowledge makes you to remain victorious all the time.

1.4 Scriptural Wisdom Answers

Moreover, you will realize that when people are amazed by your works which Your God do every day for you, people of this globe shall asked many useless questions like the Pharisees (demons) shall ask you. They will take the books of the laws of this world and they will forget that you are from the above, below is the scripture further clarifying the behaviours of people who follow the law of this world.

Luke 6:2
"And certain of the Pharisees said unto them, Why do ye that which is not lawful to do on the Sabbath days?"

Look how Jesus Christ answers in the following verse of the same chapter.

Luke 6:3
"And Jesus answering them said, Have ye not read so much as this, what David did, when himself was an hungred, and they which were with him; Luke6:4 How he went into the house of God, and did take and eat the shew-bread, and gave also to them that were with him; which it is not lawful to eat but for the priests alone?"

From this verse above Jesus replied them with what it is likely for them to remember, however, when you look in detail, the knowledge of scriptures' made Jesus to be confident in doing what He did. Meaning God allows some of the things, the fact that it happened and God allowed it, it means it can be done. Make sure all your answers and what you do is scriptural.

Let me further show you how Jesus Christ used this wisdom. When life becomes complicated, you may fall in many traps of the devil as Christians. It is important to realize that God loves us all and it is His wish and will that we <u>may</u> prosper. There are rhetorical questions you asked and you need God to answer them because of the challenges you meet. Jesus meet all of those questions from people, read the below scripture;

Luke 18:26
"And they that heard it said, Who then can be saved?"

People asked Jesus who can be saved if God is so perfect and he wants people to be as perfect as He is; see how Jesus Christ answered and obtain the wisdom origin now;

Luke 18:27
"And he said, The things which are impossible with men are possible with God."

Jesus answered with the knowledge of the Word of God through his scriptures that everything's is possible with Him. Jesus used the paradox of a rich man who gives, He said, even a camel can pass in a needle for a rich man to enter heaven. It seems impossible to human kind but to God things are possible that a camel can pass on the needle.

The paradoxical reply is very supernatural and such answers are for faith believers, this wisdom allow those with great faith to succeed. You need to have this wisdom as a Christian and know how to use it fully in day to day life. As for me, I speak impossible things and God make them possible and I know He is the One who intervened.

Notes:

CHAPTER TWO

Discernment Wisdom

2. Discernment Wisdom

To discern is to Judge, distinguish, separate, detect and to recognize any activity of a sprit and flesh. The discernment is a gift of revelation which helps you defeat the devil plans and win the battles daily. This wisdom was used by Jesus Christ a lot; I hope you will pray for this gift so that you have it, especially on the Spirit of dochimazo (Spiritual judgment). I operate on this gift a lot.

Discernment Wisdom

It should be understood by many Christians that outsiders (non-Christians or non-believers) will not understand you (you are from the above) because of the way you think and you do things. Because of your faith, you shall speak and tell people that Jesus forgives and is calling them to the Kingdom of the Lord. Some people may not understand you because they do not believe that Jesus Christ is Lords Deoxyribonucleic Acid (DNA). They will criticize you as they did to Jesus, below is how the Pharisees contempt Jesus Christ before:

Luke 5:21
"And the scribes and the Pharisees began to reason, saying, Who is this which speaketh blasphemies? Who can forgive sins, but God alone?"

From the above scripture, you will realize that the Pharisees did not believe that Jesus is the Lord and He is the Lamb of God to cleanse the sins of people of this world. Majority of people will not believe you because you will be preaching Jesus Christ whom many people did not believe in Him. Let's read below and see the wisdom of Jesus Christ answer;

Luke 5: 22-23
"But when Jesus perceived their thoughts, he answering said unto them, What reason ye in your hearts? Luke5:23 whether is easier, to say, Thy sins be forgiven thee; or to say, Rise up and walk?"

In this case, Jesus perceived (discerned) their thoughts, meaning He entered their Spirit and mind and answer them accordingly. The Spirit of discernment is very critical on such questions. You need to consult with the Holy Spirit before replying to questions you pick in the Spirit or you think of them. Jesus answered them before they speak and thus they got confused because they were not aware of why Jesus replied that way.

This wisdom will make your enemies to be confused and you will remain victorious. Most of the time, I use this wisdom in business meetings where there are investors attendance. This wisdom works for me, and I believe it can also work for you and the devil will be silent forever.

Life is not just material if it is a material. One of my friend used to say, "Life is a series of up's and down's sequence". To be specific, life is very spiritual to me. Many Christians should learn that God is Spirit, when you give in truth and in Spirit, Lord appreciate your gift because such Giving is indeed from heart, and it is a true gift that God needs. People around you may laugh at you when you give what they think is not of value. The truth and secret of giving is based on truth and Spirit. Read what Jesus Discern on wisdom of giving;

Luke 21:1-2

"And he looked up, and saw the rich men casting their gifts into the treasury. Luke21:2 And he saw also a certain poor widow casting in thither two mites."

From above Jesus looked and observed and saw two category of people; rich and poor and judged that the rich gave without heart but the poor with heart because it was her last money she had. Read below and see how Jesus the Christ answered from His discernment;

Luke 21:3-4

"And he said, Of a truth I say unto you, that this poor widow hath cast in more than they all: Luke21:4 For all these have of their abundance cast in unto the offerings of God: but she of her penury hath cast in all the living that she had."

The wisdom of giving here is that you don't give what you have but you give the last of what you have, your heart must feel touched when you give the last; nowadays Christians give what they like most because it may not be the last. The important thing we learn here is the heartfelt giving which moves the Lord. The wisdom of the answer Jesus addressed is the wisdom of God <u>moving gift</u> which happens only when your heart feel touched after giving. If many Christians' could understand this wisdom, they could have prospered long time ago.

Discernment (Answer based on follow up)

Answer based follow up discernment is the best tool I will like to see Christians using; it enables you to keeping discerning on someone Spirits or thoughts. The Pharisees said they do not know by which authority John and Jesus used to perform miracles. When you answer the question by the question, people realize that they do not know what they really want, just look below on how they replied;

Luke 20:7
"And they answered, that they could not tell whence it was."

The reply above was said after Jesus asked them a question too as a follow up. If you carefully study the verse(reply) you will realize that most enemies want what they do not know, just to catch you and to rebuke you, below is how Jesus Christ replied to them;

Luke 20:8
"And Jesus said unto them, neither tell I you by what authority I do these things."

I like this wisdom used by Jesus on this verse, Jesus used the discernment revelation (test and judge). He replied according to their answer and won His enemies. Similar, you need to apply this wisdom as Christians in daily basis to win the temptations because it will help you to be victorious. All your enemies will be under your feet if you use this wisdom as Jesus Christ our savior did.

Christians like fighting for petty and absurd things all the time. You will discover that most men and women always fight. When you look in detail what is the cause of fight, you will realize that it's very minor. Most Christian's can miss their miracle because of complain for minor things. Martha was complaining of the minor work, below read what Martha said;

Luke 10:40
"But Martha was cumbered about much serving, and came to him, and said, Lord, dost thou not care that my sister hath left me to serve alone? bid her therefore that she help me"

From the above scripture, Jesus Christ had to bring the solution to some of the petty things as the leader, just observe the wisdom of judgment Jesus answers used;

Luke 10:41-42

"And Jesus answered and said unto her, Martha, Martha, thou art careful and troubled about many things: Luke10:42 But one thing is needful: and Mary hath chosen that good part, which shall not be taken away from her."

Jesus is explaining the importance of priorities on some one life; Jesus clearly said one thing needful in life is to be with Jesus Christ while He is still around for He is about leave. When you answer people as to bring solution to them, you need to prioritize the important things first and bring best out of them. Christians must look and spent time with Jesus Christ while they can have rather than looking for petty things of this world. Christians should tap in this dimension to help others to follow Christ first. This wisdom of judgment is very important in life. You need to prioritize first and choose peace, love and God and you shall prosper.

Notes:

CHAPTER THREE

Parable Wisdom

3. Parable Wisdom

Parable means a fable, story, tale or an allegory which is an act of teaching with comparative and associative learning, and it needs a good mind and Spirit to interpret in detail of what is said, based on the current scenario at specific time. Parable Wisdom is used to give person ability (power) to comprehend the moral tale and to use it appropriately in daily life as to answer and to win the Spiritual battles. Jesus uses this wisdom a lot when defeating Satan attacks.

Parable Wisdom

If you look very carefully (observe) you will see that, in all I have written in most scriptures, people will spy and follow you on what you do in daily basis just as they followed Jesus Christ. This world will follow you on who do you meet and talk to all the time to class you. You should be very clear on your mission with God. Do not care of people perceptions, but ensure that you deliver and led them to God presence. Below is an example scripture of the how the Pharisees asked Jesus:

Luke 7:39
"Now when the Pharisee which had bidden him saw it, he spake within himself, saying, This man, if he were a prophet, would have known who and what manner of woman this is that toucheth him: for she is a sinner."

It is extremely important on how Jesus answered the above scripture. Study how He replied to this people because you shall meet such kind of people on this earth.

Luke 7-40
"And Jesus answering said unto him, Simon, I have somewhat to say unto thee. And he saith, Master, say on. Luke 7:41 There was a certain creditor which had two debtors: the one owed five hundred pence, and the other fifty. Luke 7:42 And when they had nothing to pay, he frankly forgave them both. Tell me therefore, which of them will love him most?"

Jesus wanted Simon to have a heart of judgment (discernment wisdom), that is, the importance of forgiving others without measurement of their sins. God will forgive us without judgment as long as we repent.

Let me further explicit this wisdom of parable answering of Jesus to you. You see, people normally enjoy searching for many reasons of why things happen the way they happen to Christians, and when they get a factual answer, they will try by all means to get the loop hole for them, trying to escape or justifying from the fact, just as it happened to Jesus Christ;

Luke 10: 29
"But he, willing to justify himself, said unto Jesus, And who is my neighbour?"

The most important fact to have in your mind as the Christians is that; you will find individuals who will always defend them on everything especially during Evangelism era. Look below on how Jesus replied to them in wisdom.

Luke 10: 30-37
"And Jesus answering said, A certain man went down from Jerusalem to Jericho, and fell among thieves, which stripped him of his raiment, and wounded him, and departed, leaving him half dead..."

If you read the verse above till the end, you will realize that Jesus answered the above question in a parable way for easy understanding of the defender. If you meet some challenges' as a Christian, give out question-thought phrase in a parable way for the person you are explaining to understand much better. These can be used in explanation of the Word of God to those who do not understand the word of God through their defensive manner. This wisdom will help you in your business, career and in day to day life for your survival.

Let me continue pointing more examples of the application of parable wisdom of answering. As Christian, you need to screen people you communicate with, not all people shall understand you, but those close to God or those close to you in Spirit. At times, not all information should be given to everybody but to those ready to use it. Some information belongs to the children of God not to foreigners'. Below is the question asked by Peter to Jesus?

Luke 12: 41
"Then Peter said unto him, Lord, speakest thou this parable unto us, or even to all?"

Peter ask Jesus the question because, he believed that not all people can understand what Jesus is saying, meaning only those with revelation and close to Jesus can understand what he said. Read below how Jesus replied;

Luke 12:42
"And the Lord said, Who then is that faithful and wise steward, whom his lord shall make ruler over his household, to give them their portion of meat in due season?"

If you observe the nature of the answer, is the parable answer that Jesus can speak certain issues to his faithful people, who understand Him better and such can eat and life with the master. Meaning, He spoke in parables just for those who are close to Him in Spirit to understand and to use the Word for their success.

In life, as a Christian, God may choose you to uplift His children in many ways, you need to have wisdom to make your fellow Christian to have a good life, and make those evil to continue doing bad or else they will take what belongs to children of God, so speaking in a parable way shall help them. I pray that this wisdom manifest in your life in Jesus name!

parable rebuking wisdom answers

When you speak and show the manifestation of the mighty Lord you serve, majority of people will not like it. You need to boast and praise your God, because He is powerful and Mighty. It is this time people will attack you, especially if more people follows your God. Jesus Christ met such situations. Look below what He met;

Luke 19:39
"And some of the Pharisees from among the multitude said unto him, Master, rebuke thy disciples."

From the scripture, the Pharisees wanted the disciples of Jesus to stop praising their God, in-fact they said Jesus must rebuke His disciplines, it is very interesting to read how Jesus replied to them;

Luke19:40
"And he answered and said unto them, I tell you that, if these should hold their peace, the stones would immediately cry out."

Jesus answered them with parable wisdom, He said the stones will immediately cry out and worship. Meaning Jesus is saying God need to be worshipped by nature. Jesus did not say they are wrong, but He spoke of stones ability to worship if His disciplines could stop. The wisdom we learn here is; make people to follow you without directly attacking them, but answer them in a way they feel accommodated. This wisdom keeps followers while teaching them the truth, many leaders need this wisdom to keep church, companies and organization running well.

When you follow Jesus, the Babylonia people shall trace your life just as the born-again are being traced daily. Major Prophets like Jesus are criticized all the times, because of different Holy life they live compared to the earthly life. Expect the same to happen to you as you follow Jesus. Let's read below on how the Scribes and Pharisees murmured:

Luke 5:30
"But their scribes and Pharisees murmured against his disciples, saying, why do ye eat and drink with publicans and sinners?"

Like I said before in this book, when you born-again, people will look on who do you eat with, walk with, and so on, and they shall complain on how you do things yet yourself you are not worried of their life, do not worry about such people. Just look below on how Jesus Christ answered the Scribes:

Luke 5:31-32
"And Jesus answering said unto them, they that are whole need not a physician; but they that are sick. Luke 5:32 I came not to call the righteous, but sinners to repentance."

Jesus simply says, those who are with Christ like me and you do not need a physician because Christ lives in them. However, those who need Jesus need to be healed. This simply fulfills the verse which says I can do all things with Christ who dwells in me. We are here to deliver the sinners, and for them to repent with the name of Jesus just as it is happening today. This wisdom of rebuking people needs confidence. You need to be confident as a Christian that there is life after death and people should repent. This wisdom will help you to remember that sinners are not allowed in heaven, in fact they are prohibited.

Notes:

_____

_____

_____

_____

_____

_____

_____

_____

_____

_____

_____

_____

_____

_____

_____

_____

CHAPTER FOUR

Nothing Wisdom

4. Nothing Wisdom

Nothing Wisdom is also known as the nil, unknown, zero, and or nobody wisdom of winning against evil spirits but gaining good things. This wisdom involve the strict observation of events while very quiet "be quite phenomenon". There is a time Jesus applied this one. It is one of my favorite wisdom and I am still practicing this wisdom currently.

Nothing Answer Wisdom

There will be times majority of people will tempt you and expect you to show that you are the child of God. People will expect miracles, sings and wonders from you and you need to be very intelligent on how to deal with such matters. Herod expected the same when he met our Lord Jesus the Christ. Look the scripture below;

Luke 23:8
"And when Herod saw Jesus, he was exceeding glad: for he was desirous to see him of a long season, because he had heard many things of him; and he hoped to have seen some miracle done by him."

As I mentioned, as you grow spiritually and the Lord Grace is upon you, people will follow you. I like the way Jesus responded, read below:

Luke 23:9
"Then he questioned with him in many words; but he answered him nothing."

I like this verse so much, and the nothing wisdom on this verse. Jesus kept quiet "He answered him nothing". Yes, it is quite important to keep quite at times as a child of God. Nothing wisdom can help you to win many of your enemies through quietness.

The bible says, even the Christians will be taken to leaders and those taking to leaders to be persecuted shall remain silent, but the Holy Spirit will utter on their behalf. This wisdom is very good when you are new at the place or on the hostile situation and you want familiarize yourself with it. I used this wisdom when I have visited places and business to orient myself. I also apply this wisdom when the place is a bit freezing or hostile. Keeping quite helps me a lot.

Notes:

_____

_____

_____

_____

_____

_____

_____

_____

_____

_____

_____

_____

_____

_____

_____

_____

_____

CHAPTER FIVE

Prophetic Wisdom

5. Prophetic Wisdom

Prophetic can mean Foretelling, forewarning, Oracular, farsighted, divinatory and or visionary. Above all things, prophetic is spiritual and prophetic movement is extremely powerful. The prophetic wisdom is one of the dangerous wisdom. It can be a gift of speech and Christians should desire this wisdom in their daily life.

Prophetic Wisdom Answers

As Christians, some people will understand you much better. Most people will later follow you and see exactly who you are; you should not be pompous when people follow you as man of God, rather explain what they see in you, listen and appreciate what they say. See scripture below;

Luke 11: 27

"And it came to pass, as he spake these things, a certain woman of the company lifted up her voice, and said unto him, Blessed is the womb that bare thee, and the paps which thou hast sucked".

From the above scripture, we see people following Jesus starting to complement him, about how blessed is His mother, however just learn how Jesus replied to the followers.

Luke 11:28
"But he said, Yea rather, blessed are they that hear the word of God, and keep it".

Here is the Wisdom of Jesus Christ from the complements by the followers; He said blessed is they that hear the Word of God and Keep it, meaning that Jesus puts God first in all the things He does, He put the Word of God first above the complements and encourages people to know the Word of God and to keep it. As a Christian, encourage people who follow you personally to follow the Word of God and keep it. Do not feel pride and forget to praise the Lord of heavenly host. This is the wisdom to gain anointing, favour and Grace from the Lord our savior. This wisdom is needed by men of God mostly.

Moreover, I wonder if you ever felt like me on this issue; Every time I think of the coming of Christ (rupture), I feel happy and at the same time I feel challenged, the reason being that; there are many prophets and some are fakes. The question is how many Christians' are lost?. You need to look as a Christian and you can see all the prophetic words and events passing by today symbolizing the coming of the Son of God. It is interesting to read below the question Jesus Christ was asked about His coming, see the verse below;

Luke 21:7
"And they asked him, saying, Master, but when shall these things be? and what sign will there be when these things shall come to pass?"

The disciplines asked Jesus of the signs which can be shown to them, as they want to see, prepare and get ready for the coming of Christ. Look carefully the way Jesus Christ is answering the question.

Luke 21:8

"And he said, Take heed that ye be not deceived: for many shall come in my name, saying, I am Christ; and the time draweth near: go ye not therefore after them."

The first point Jesus says here is; be careful not to be deceived, meaning people are going to be deceived because many shall come with His name. The wisdom Jesus is expressing here is, check first the life of the man of God, and listen to your inner man before you jump into conclusion of following Jesus through him. Generally, in life we should not act abruptly but we need to observe first, so that we can take the decision. I advise many of Christians to be aware of this wisdom in daily life applications.

Prophetic wisdom is a need to each Christian. There are many questions we ask ourselves especially after the man of God gave us prophetic instructions. In prophetic ministry it is allowed to ask for further clarity, however, at times submission comes first. Study the verse below very carefully and see how this wisdom is applied to you as a Christian.

Luke 22:9

"And they said unto him, where wilt thou that we prepare?"

The disciplines had to ask Jesus for the right place of preparations, below is how Jesus Christ answered prophetically;

Luke 22:10

"And he said unto them, Behold, when ye are entered into the city, there shall a man meet you, bearing a pitcher of water; follow him into the house where he entereth in."

This is the prophetic answer, Jesus says behold, meaning observe and follow the man you will meet, Jesus explains how the man will look like. Immediately He gave His disciplines what to do. Jesus used the prophetic wisdom to answer the disciplines. In life, some answers' you need to produce should be prophetic answers. This wisdom I use it when I motivate the workers in my organization. What usually surprise me is that; all I said will pass exactly as I answered. Prophetic answers gives hope and God initiate them for His people because of great faith they entailed. Use this wisdom in your daily life. Declare and decree victory against evil spirits.

Notes:

CHAPTER SIX

Factual or True Wisdom

6. Factual or True Wisdom

Factual means something realistic, truthful, genuine and honest pertaining any statement or for a particular activity. Now, a factual wisdom means the perception of what is realistic. This wisdom is very interesting because you speak the truth and every person shall understand your say.

Factual Answers

Like in other previous paragraphs, you will realize that, Jesus had been followed by the Pharisees to find out how they can criticize Him in everything He does. Christians also have to go through such behaviours' like their Master Jesus Christ as to fulfill that they follow Him.

Luke 11:38
"And when the Pharisee saw it, he marveled that he had not first washed before dinner."

People will look what you do, and speak amongst themselves so that you may hear what they think of you. You need to follow how Jesus approached such attacks or challenges, use the skill Jesus used and you shall win, below is how Jesus replies to them;

Luke 11:39

"And the Lord said unto him, Now do ye Pharisees make clean the outside of the cup and the platter; but your inward part is full of ravening and wickedness".

Jesus Christ explains that most (people) can hide themselves by portraying themselves to be good people yet their inner is very bad, Jesus had to state a fact so that the Pharisees can be quite. At times as a Christian, you need to state the fact so that the attack can stop.

When you use this factual wisdom, you need to have a Spirit of discernment since it is very important to Christians, because some of the demons can attack you through actions not through communication; to have spiritual sensors is very good, you need to pray for that. Some people can speak through actions. In Jesus time, Christian's were doing some actions which would make Jesus Christ to answer without their verbal communication. Look below the following verse;

Luke 13: 1

"There were present at that season some that told him of the Galilaeans, whose blood Pilate had mingled with their sacrifices."

Christians stated on the above verse came to Jesus and told him about the Galatians Pilate killed because of sins. They believed that there is a sin worse that the other, look below how Jesus Christ replied to them:

Luke 13:2-3

"And Jesus answering said unto them, Suppose ye that these Galilaeans were sinners above all the Galilaeans, because they suffered such things? Luke13:3 I tell you, Nay: but, except ye repent, ye shall all likewise perish."

Jesus replied to them that all sins are sins to God, and God does not meet with sins completely. Jesus here, call a spade a spade, He did not hesitate to give a factual answer to the Christians'. In life you need to have time to speak facts, especially on Godly things on people deserving to know, this wisdom helps a lot of people to solve many challenging situation in their life. I hope you copy this behavour of Jesus Christ.

Still on factual wisdom, some people will ask you questions which need truth, because they believe in you on the things of the Lord, or in anything they trust you on. It is important not to serve or to justify the answers but to be factual so that people should know the reality. Jesus at time, His followers would ask him questions looking for the truth which is direct and factual. Below is the example of verse for such questions you will meet.

Luke 13: 23
"Then said one unto him, Lord, are there few that be saved?"

This question above is truly making sense, and Jesus had to answer the person with the fact for the person knowledge sake. Let's look how He replied to the above question.

Luke 13: 24
"Strive to enter in at the strait gate: for many, I say unto you, will seek to enter in, and shall not be able."

Jesus replied to the Christian with a factual answer, that he needs to enter through a straight gate. Meaning, God cannot be cheated by people; the best way is to do right with Gods' people for God. As Christians, we need a special wisdom to pick in the Spirit people who seek knowledge because they want to know more in details. This wisdom you need it because other people can take you astray in life while others seeks the truth from you. Just follow how Lord Jesus Christ used a factual wisdom of answering the Questions.

As a child of God, It is also important to realize that some enemies can contempt you when you speak the facts. Majority of people live material life and they belief that money is everything. They do not know money is added when you follow Christ. Facts are needed, as they are good to be told to people seeking knowledge. Look how Jesus was contempt;

Luke 16:13-14

"No servant can serve two masters: for either he will hate the one, and love the other; or else he will hold to the one, and despise the other. Ye cannot serve God and mammon. Luke16:14 And the Pharisees also, who were covetous, heard all these things: and they derided him."

From the above scripture, you will realize what Jesus was saying, the Pharisees we laughing at him in scorn, but observe the wisdom of him responding to that;

Luke 16:15-16

"And he said unto them, Ye are they which justify yourselves before men; but God knoweth your hearts: for that which is highly esteemed among men is abomination in the sight of God. Luke16:16 The law and the prophets were until John: since that time the kingdom of God is preached, and every man presseth into it."

Jesus spoke the fact to the Pharisees that they display their material than following God truly and spiritually. Their outer look good, yet the inner is darkness. Majority of people deserves to be told the truth, especially when they be-little you on God issues, as Christians we need to speak out the facts against scorners until they know the truth. Use the wisdom to win your enemies fighting you. I see the results of this wisdom especially in business. I speak the fact and the truth and my business rivals usually fail and God normally turn me victorious because I am following Jesus Wisdom.

In life, various challenges can attack you severally; you need to have wisdom of how to tackle them. Jesus went through similar situation, one of the question He were asked severally as a repeat is below:

Luke 18:18
"And a certain ruler asked him, saying, Good Master, what shall I do to inherit eternal life?"

If you carefully read the above question, the ruler asked Jesus Christ, it is the question of inheriting eternal life; notice the key important word in the verse, the word "Good". Below is how Jesus replied;

Luke 18:19
"And Jesus said unto him, Why callest thou me good? none is good, save one, that is, God."

The way Jesus replied to the person is based on the interpretation of the word "good", if the ruler asked the question without adding the word good, Jesus could have answered him, however, Jesus has the wisdom of listening the core word in the communication and directly responded to it. If we can be able to pick the core word as people speak or attack us and replied accordingly, we as Christians can win every battles, tenders and business deals because of the way we answer. Many Christians fail to secure businesses and deals because of lack of wisdom of answering questions. Receive this wisdom now!

Like I said in previous verses, there will be real people who will be seeking to know the truth of God, such people deserves to know the truth and we need to tell them the truth all the time, so that they learn more about spiritual things, below is an example of the question Jesus Christ met;

Luke 20:21-22
"And they asked him, saying, Master, we know that thou sayest and teachest rightly, neither acceptest thou the person of any, but teachest the way of God truly: Luke 20:22 Is it lawful for us to give tribute unto Caesar, or no?"

When you study the verse above, you will realize that people wanted the right way of doing things from the teacher, it is different to those who call him "good". Thus Jesus had to answer them according to the need of the question, analyze the wisdom below of how Jesus replied;

Luke 20:23-25
"But he perceived their craftiness, and said unto them, Why tempt ye me? Luke 20:24 Shew me a penny. Whose image and superscription hath it? They answered and said, Caesar's. Luke 20:25 And he said unto them, Render therefore unto Caesar the things which be Caesar's, and unto God the things which be God's."

Look very carefully how Jesus Christ replied. The people wanted to know the truth though they were tempting Jesus. Jesus realizes their craftiness but decided to answer them accordingly, this wisdom of answering the fact by fact is very dangerous, I will like you to learn this wisdom since it will help you, especially in courts of law. You will see that Jesus Christ answers are very critical and are needed in life. Prophets like this wisdom so much.

If you may look on most of the verses on this book, people were asking if Jesus is the Son of God. The question is; why they were asking such questions?. Time is coming, people will constantly ask you of who are you. It is very important to answer them again and again with confidence and with facts. Look below how Pilate asked Jesus;

Luke 23:3
"And Pilate asked him, saying, Art thou the King of the Jews? And he answered him and said, Thou sayest it."

Jesus answered Pilate by saying you have already said it. Jesus knew that He was the Son of God and He was not shy about it because of confidence and covenant with His father. This wisdom I pray that you always tap in this dimension all the time. For this wisdom to manifest in your life, you need to hear the word of God frequently. This wisdom moves God because God needs people who are not ashamed of Him, God need people who speak about Him publicly. Tap in this wisdom of answering questions. Normally your "YES" should be "YES" and your "NO" should be your "NO". Jesus answered with the fact and Pilate had no other way to asked Jesus.

If you may look very deep, most of Jesus answers' were factual, because a fact is a truth and Jesus is the Truth Himself. Let me set you one more verse where Jesus applied factual wisdom.

When most people realized that you belong to God as a Christian, many will follow your God and believe in you. Many will take you as their father and their mother and they will cry when you leave them. It happened with the multitudes of Jesus Christ followers. See the verse below;

Luke 23:27
"And there followed him a great company of people, and of women, which also bewailed and lamented him".

Jesus discerned in their hearts and replied to them in a special way as they were weeping and lamenting. Observe the way Jesus answers' people. Observe the wisdom of His answer;

Luke 23:28
"But Jesus turning unto them said, Daughters of Jerusalem, weep not for me, but weep for yourselves, and for your children."

Jesus said do not weep for me but weep for your daughters. Jesus knows His objective, and He was fine because He is the Lamb of God to cleanse our sins, however, majority of daughters in Jerusalem denied Him and refused Him. Jesus is simply saying, cry for your children for they will need the word and to experience God while I am gone. This wisdom,

I normally use it at the company I am working at. I normally tell my workers that they will know what they used to have until they lose me.

Tell people about the truth of who you are. This will make your bosses not to expel you because they know who you are. You will be surprised to know that, their business is succeeding because of you. In fact if they expel you, their business will die.

Jesus had people whom He was crucified with, one these people believed that Jesus is the Lord and if Jesus can remember Him, he will be saved. In life, there will be people who will support you, and you need to remember them when God gives you kingship and blessings. Most men of God forgot to give blessings to those who went through difficult times with, below is what Jesus heard and understood from the person He was crucified with. Read below;

Luke 23:42
"And he said unto Jesus, Lord; remember me when thou comest into thy kingdom."

The person asked Jesus simple things. But the word to "remember" in the verse above is very deep. Let's see how Jesus Christ replied him.

Luke 23:43
"And Jesus said unto him, Verily I say unto thee, To day shalt thou be with me in paradise".

Jesus gave the man an assurance that today they shall be in paradise together. Jesus had the wisdom of assurance and of knowing the wisdom of blessing those you went with in difficult times. This wisdom is very important. As Christians, do not divorce one another or forget your prayer partners when God blesses you. God loves those who "remember". This wisdom increases your personal and makes God to gives you more authority and grace, thus I encourage most people to remember on how to tap on this dimension of wisdom and anointing.

Moreover, you will realize that in life most people when they realize that you bare the marks of Jesus Christ, they will follow you and surrender themselves to your Lord of heavenly host. They will finally speak of your God, they will repent from bad awkward situations, just as recorded on the verse below;

Luke 19:8
"And Zacchaeus stood, and said unto the Lord; Behold, Lord, the half of my goods I give to the poor; and if I have taken anything from any man by false accusation, I restore him fourfold."

From the above verse, we read that Zacchaeus gave half of the riches to God, and restored (repent) materials he took by force from various people. Look below on how Jesus replied, analyze the wisdom;

Luke 19:9
"And Jesus said unto him, This day is salvation come to this house, forasmuch as he also is a son of Abraham."

The wisdom Jesus replies to the above situation is to praise God and that there is celebration in heaven during repentance. The wisdom Jesus expresses here is that, everything good, especially when a person accepts the Lord and repent, it is not by your own power but by the power of the Lord. Learn to give credit to the lord not your own self. Remember you are the vessel of the Lord.

Jesus was asked several times whether He is indeed a son of God by people, this is because they did not believe Him, and they did not know the Word of God very well. As you bare the marks of Jesus Christ, majority of people will ask you so many questions on whether you are the child of God or what. Jesus met the similar situation, read the verse below and also finds out how he responded;

Luke 22:70
"Then said they all, Art thou then the Son of God? And he said unto them, Ye say that I am."

Jesus simply said; you are rightly saying I am the Son of God and ofcourse "I am". One of the surprising and shocking times is when Christians deny that they are children of God because of earthly situation. When you fully know who you are, you will have wisdom of confidence in you. This wisdom of factualism give boldness and people will see Jesus Christ in you. I pray every day for Christian's to tap in this dimension of full demonstrative characters' toward the love of Jesus Christ. The demonstration of faith in Jesus Christ gives the wisdom of facts. Receive this wisdom now!!

Notes:

CHAPTER SEVEN

Question by Question Wisdom

7. Question by Question Wisdom

A "Question" is defined as a general word which can be used to explain inquiry, enquiry, query and or a problem. The wisdom of question to question answering means you answer a problem by a problem, a query by a query. There will be a communication but without a solution, yet sense and comprehensive message is been clearly conveyed.

Questions by question Answering

People who are tracking and tracing you will ask you funny things same way Jesus experienced. The question is; why are they following your life? The answer is simply that you are of Jesus Christ, thus you need to follow His steps. The scripture below further shows how persistent were the Scribes and Pharisees.

Luke 5:33
"And they said unto him, why do the disciples of John fast often, and make prayers, and likewise the disciples of the Pharisees; but thine eat and drink?"

Let's understand the deep wisdom and revelation of Jesus Christ on the above questions by the scribes and Pharisees. below is how Jesus Christ answered;

Luke 5:34
"And he said unto them, Can ye make the children of the bride-chamber fast, while the bridegroom is with them".

Looking in detail the wisdom of this answer by question, we realize that Jesus says, I am the Lord and I live with my people "Emmanuel", so why should they fast yet I am with them?. So on this world, you need to realize that Jesus lives in you and you need to have a Holy life above all things, then Jesus shall be with you. The fact Jesus answered them with a description questions, the Pharisees stopped asking. Some answers you should give in life as a Christians are as Jesus answered.

Jesus liked this wisdom of answering a question by question so much, and as a Christian you will meet many challenges especially while teaching the children of God about the word of God. In such people, there are those who will intimidate you and make you to lose focus on the teaching of the word. The same thing happens to you in life. Jesus Christ encountered the same situation, read the scripture below:

Luke 12: 13
"And one of the company said unto him, Master, speak to my brother, that he divide the inheritance with me."

If you will carefully follow the scripture above, you will realize that, the person was just disturbing Jesus, and because of the discernment, Jesus answered him with the question, read the scripture below;

Luke 12: 14
"And he said unto him, Man, who made me a judge or a divider over you?"

For the answer to be clear to you, when you read a verse below this scripture, you will realize that Jesus continues teaching, meaning Jesus answers the question with the question and He defeated the enemy simply by that wisdom, meaning in life, there will be some questions to take you out of the focus especially in spreading the word of God, you will need to be careful on how to handle such issues. The wisdom of answering the question with the question is useful to make you victorious in such challenges. Some attacks you will meet in life, you just need to apply this wisdom as Jesus used to implement it.

When you have tapped and you are aware this wisdom, people can make you feel uncomfortable to praise, and to do the work your God, because of their various beliefs. This situation has made majority of Christians to lack confidence doing and in speaking the truth of the Word of God to others. Look the scriptures below on how also Jesus felt the situation too;

Luke 14:1-2

"And it came to pass, as he went into the house of one of the chief Pharisees to eat bread on the Sabbath day, that they watched him. Luke14:2 And, behold, there was a certain man before him which had the dropsy".

Jesus asked the Pharisees about the past situation, when they confronted Him on healing people on the Sabath day. See how Jesus corrected the Pharisees behavior and belief through the wisdom of question answering;

Luke 14:3

And Jesus answering spake unto the lawyers and Pharisees, saying, Is it lawful to heal on the Sabbath day?

I like this wisdom and many times I apply this one. People can do things when they favour them but while the issue does not favour them, they ignore it or contest against it. Jesus asked them question because they needed a special help from Him, however, it happened that it was on the Sabbath day which they believed it was unlawful to heal a person. The question wisdom forcefully turns the Pharisees mind-set towards the new belief and towards the new system. As a Christian, you must apply this wisdom frequently, especially toward your enemies. Copy and apply this knowledge.

Like any other wisdom, I encourage you to practice this wisdom and see its effects. People we live with them have various mindset and thoughts; some may come to you to seek help. Jesus had some of his followers looking for miracles following him, look below how they spoke to Jesus;

Luke 17:13-14

"And they lifted up their voices, and said, Jesus, Master, have mercy on us. Luke17:14 And when he saw them, he said unto them, Go shew yourselves unto the priests. And it came to pass, that, as they went, they were cleansed.

People call Jesus for help and they were given a prophetic instruction by Jesus. However, they did not come back all of them to thank him, read below how Jesus replied to them when He saw them and observe the wisdom of questions;

Luke 17:15, 17

"And Jesus answering said, were there not ten cleansed? but where are the nine?"

When Jesus realized that they did not return, he asked them a question by answer; by saying were there not ten? This wisdom of asking a question by the question make the people and enemies to be shaken, because they know that you are sharp and you can remember everything. This wisdom I like it so much because it makes people to believe in you and to know that you are responsible. People cannot just lie and destroy your properties because they know you will ask them the answer. I found this wisdom working for me so much in Organization. I hope it can work for you too and make you a prosperous Christian.

Allow me to show you as much as I can the application of the wisdom of question answer and you will see how our Lord Jesus Christ used it.

On this earth, people will ask you very funny questions on how your God operate, if you are not carefully, you can be trapped because God is unexplainable most of the times. Jesus met such questions; see the example of the verse quoted;

Luke 20:2
"And spake unto him, saying, Tell us, by what authority doest thou these things? or who is he that gave thee this authority?"

Studying the nature of the question, they ask where Jesus got the authority to do miracles. Major 1 (My spiritual Father) faces such questions too and I believe you do go through such questions as a Christian too. Let's see how Jesus the Christ responded to such questions;

Luke 20:3-4
"And he answered and said unto them, I will also ask you one thing; and answer me: Luke20:4 The baptism of John, was it from heaven, or of men?"

Jesus answered the question by the question, the wisdom of this answer is based on what people believed on before, and Jesus want to know where is the difference between Him and John according to the Pharisees. They believed John to the extent that they belief that they should repent and be baptized by John. You see, in life, they shall ask you such questions as a believer; the wisdom is; take all what they believe on and apply your current concept. At times you need to have the wisdom of answering the question by the question to defeat your attacks or enemies. Adapt this wisdom and use it in your daily situation and life.

Majority of Christians answers every question. Some questions do not need an explanation to you as a Christian but a deep revelation on how to answer them. People can even ask you your name (position) just to be-little you and make you feel weak. Jesus our Lord and savior went through the same contempt, below is how Jesus Christ met such challenges;

Luke 22:67
"Art thou the Christ? tell us. And he said unto them, If I tell you, ye will not believe"

From the above Scripture, Jesus was asked who He is, and the question look like a special temptation. Below is how Jesus Christ answered the question;

Luke 22:68
"And if I also ask you, ye will not answer me, nor let me go."

Look the answer of Jesus very close, He asked a question before even answering the people. The wisdom here is; when you ask or answer the enemy with the question, a big confusion starts and stir in the sprint and mind of such person. People will come and ask you funny questions. You need to have a good way to respond to them. Ask them a question before answering, and see if they will follow their plans. Several times, my father Major 1, also ask the interviewers questions during the interviews before answering. You will agree with me that, the interviewers' normally get confused and he will win the case, discussion or allegations. Do the same too and your life will never be the same again.

Notes:

CHAPTER EIGHT

Worship Wisdom

8. Worship wisdom

A word "Worship" can be defined as adoration, love, devotion, respect, reverence and or adulation. Worship is from Greek word meaning to lick you master's feet lying flat on the ground. Now, Worship wisdom is the dimension of perception on adulation towards certain person, act, behavior or animal.

Worship Wisdom

The truth Many Christians do not know is that, Devil deceives them with what belongs to them. Jesus was attacked by devil with what belongs to Him. It has to be clear that the cause of the war is the competition of worship between Satan and God. Jesus is Lord, meaning that, the world belongs to Jesus the Son of God, nevertheless, let's read the scripture below and learn more on this wisdom.

Luke 4:6
**"And the devil said unto him, All this power
will I give thee, and the glory of them: for that is
delivered unto me; and to whomsoever I will I give**

it.Luke4:7 If thou therefore wilt worship me, all shall be thine".

It is very important to study the way Jesus answered the devil. Jesus understands very well that the devil wanted Him to worship him. Demons makes many Christians to worship them, however, there is a special answer from Jesus Christ from the below scripture, study it carefully and see the deep origin of the wisdom;

Luke4:8
"And Jesus answered and said unto him, Get thee behind me, Satan: for it is written, Thou shalt worship the Lord thy God, and him only shalt thou serve".

Jesus Christ rebuked the devil with his name and codes the scripture, meaning Jesus knew the Word of God and He answered the Devil with the Word of God, meaning the word of God is the powerful weapon or wisdom to defeat the devil. Worshipping is the important fact in the Kingdom of God and in the Kingdom of darkness. It is importance to rebuke spirits looking for your worship. You need to worship only the Spirit of God.

Notes:

CHAPTER NINE

Unquestionable Wisdom

9. Unquestionable Wisdom

To be Unquestionable is to be undisputable, incontestable, and undeniable or to be conclusive. Unquestionable Wisdom is the degree of perception you cannot doubt. This wisdom is self-explanatory and self-convincing, there is no need of evidence, and practical actions are only touchable proof.

When you became born-again, many people will tell you that; you do sin, and most Christians are attacked by people based on old issues or with what they think you are. Look these verse below and realize how Jesus Christ was approached be the devil.

Luke 4:22
"And all bare him witness, and wondered at the gracious words which proceeded out of his mouth. And they said, Is not this Joseph's son?"

The above scripture clearly indicates that Jesus was speaking Words of wisdom, meaning if you belong to Jesus Christ, your words must surprise a lot of people who think they know you. I like the way Jesus Christ answers this question:

Luke 4:23-24

"And he said unto them, Ye will surely say unto me this proverb, Physician, heal thyself: whatsoever we have heard done in Capernaum, do also here in thy country. Luke 4:24 And he said, Verily I say unto you, No prophet is accepted in his own country"

It should be clear that many people who know you, or who raise you in your area, became very difficult to follow Jesus through you. Jesus prophesied that, it will be so at your home area. This implies that, **as** Christians we should work harder to change people mind-set at our vicinity to follow us as we follow Jesus Christ. The wisdom of the answer above is based in psychological alertness of who you are.

Furthermore, you will learn that most Christians focus on material things, when Christian speaks about the Lord Goodness and mercy, people will ask you about earthly material things and their desire. I like the prophetic ministry so much, because material things happen in seconds, as Christians we feel challenged by such questions from people. Similarly, Jesus Christ met similar scenarios, study carefully the verses below and see the wisdom of His answer;

Luke 18:22-23

"Now when Jesus heard these things, he said unto him, Yet lackest thou one thing: sell all that thou hast, and distribute unto the poor, and thou shalt have treasure in heaven: and come, follow me. Luke18:23 And when he heard this, he was very sorrowful: for he was very rich."

Jesus tell the man that real riches are found in heaven, remember the Word of God says, seek first the kingdom of God and the rest shall be added, meaning the sentence "follow me" is very prophetic to us as Christians to follow Jesus. We could understand that people did not understand the kingdom of God, that's why it was difficult to comprehend what Jesus said and who He was.

There are something's which are discerned by the Lord mighty to us as people. We need to do certain things because God told us to do them. It can be direct or through a man of God. What is important is to submit and do what the Spirit says.

Luke 19:31
"And if any man ask you, Why do ye loose him? thus shall ye say unto him, Because the Lord hath need of him."

On the same verse, Jesus told the man He sent to say the Lord need the donkey. Be careful, Jesus did not say Jesus needs it but the Lord needs it. When the King of Kings needs something, you just do. The wisdom of the answer was based on time saving and command execution. The world call it dictator, but the wisdom can be used to speed than arguing, to do what God wants than requesting people thoughts. I usually apply this wisdom when God has spoken to me. At that time, I do not need a person thoughts, plan or wishes. I just execute the command as it is. This wisdom does not always apply and you need to be careful on which places you use the wisdom.

Furthermore, when things happen around you, you will face situations you will not understand as a Christian and normally flash will take over. You will act abruptly without thinking, many of this scenarios happened even to people closest to you. Below is what happened in front of Jesus Christ;

Luke 22:50
"And one of them smote the servant of the high priest, and cut off his right ear."

Like I said above, the verse shows the man who acted without deep thinking to protect his Master Jesus Christ. It will be surprising to see how Jesus Christ answered him, read the verse below.

Luke 22:51
"And Jesus answered and said, Suffer ye thus far. And he touched his ear, and healed him."

Look carefully the wisdom of Jesus Christ answer basis, Jesus knew that it was His time to fulfill the need of His father (Lord) and He fix the ear of the enemy. He knows that, the sufferings are ending to people on that day. As a Christian you need to know your objective. Enemies will think they are affecting you negatively, and they will only realize that they have made you stronger in the Lord. What gave Jesus strength is that; He knows who He is, what He is here for. He knew His objectives'. The wisdom here is a "targeted brave confident answer" because Jesus knew His objectives and could see His fulfillment of His victory. Don't be shaken as a Christian, use the wisdom of targeted brave confident answer".

Notes:

_____

_____

_____

_____

_____

_____

_____

_____

_____

_____

_____

_____

_____

_____

_____

_____

_____

_____

CHAPTER TEN

Rebuking Wisdom

10. Rebuking Wisdom

Rebuking means an action process of telling-off, reprimanding, criticizing, scolding and or reproving the information, act or behavour of some activity that time. Rebuking Wisdom is the judgment perception of when and how to rebuke someone to win him or her in your site.

Rebuking Wisdom

It should be understood by most Christians that, a devil shall not appear in front of you to tempt you, but a devil normally come to you in human spirit, either your friend or person very close to you. Read the scripture below and see how Jesus Christ was attacked by the demon.

Luke 4:34
"Saying Let us alone; what have we to do with thee,
thou Jesus of Nazareth? art thou come to destroy us?
I know thee who thou art; the Holy One of God".

From the above Scripture, we understand that people were challenging Jesus Christ and be-little him by words of disgrace that He calls Himself a Holy one of God. Prophetically, majority of people will not trust you easily and the demon will attack you through such people. It is imperative to understand wisdom of Jesus Christ to such foolish questions, see below how Jesus Christ applied the rebuking wisdom;

Luke 4:35
"And Jesus rebuked him, saying, Hold thy peace, and come out of him. And when the devil had thrown him in the midst, he came out of him, and hurt him not".

From the above Scripture we realized the gift of revelation (discernment), that Jesus stopped the man from speaking and cast out a demon out. Many Christians argue and have conflicts with their fellow church-mate or parents, because of the lack of this wisdom from God. It is important to first ask yourselves whether; is it the person or the demonic spirit speaking? Then you can answer the question very clearly. Rebuke people on facts, it will be easy for you to discern very easy. I like using the wisdom at our church. I rebuke them fast or listen if it's the church mate speaking or a demon speaking. If it is a demon speaking, I will internally rebuke and pray that; the demon should go out. Use this wisdom it will help most of your church mate who can be possessed by any demonic spirit.

The world followers will be against spiritual people proving the fact that the flesh and Spirit are antagonistic. Jesus was always asked questions as to tempt him by the law students who studied bible. The same things shall happen in your life and you will need to understand that we shall meet such challenges like him.

Luke 11:45
"Then answered one of the lawyers, and said unto him, Master, thus saying thou reproachest us also."

From the above scripture, we see that the student was just challenging Jesus and Jesus had to answer him in this way;

Luke 11: 46
"And he said, Woe unto you also, ye lawyers! for ye lade men with burdens grievous to be borne, and ye

yourselves touch not the burdens with one of your fingers."

Jesus rebuked the person by telling him that he cannot do anything, however they speak too much. Pharisees and earthly people of this world shall challenge you with talks. As a Christian demonstrate power of evidence, demonstrate to people as the way to answer some of the questions. Jesus told them face to face, fact to fact that they cannot do anything. At times, you need to copy exactly how Jesus replied and relate to people. That's the meaning of this book. Real man of God copy this behaviour of not caring what people think, but they care on what God says. Rebuke people in life and protect God. You shall be saved by God if you apply this wisdom in life.

Notes:

CHAPTER ELEVEN

Evidence Wisdom

11. Evidence Wisdom

The word "evidence" means a sign, indication, signal, mark, proof, confirmation and or substantial point one is doing as to win his attackers' or non-believers on a particular issue or matter. The wisdom is a high dimension normally seen in prophets of our generation. Evidence wisdom is similar to the unquestionable wisdom. No one questions the answer. One plus one equals two (1+1=$\underline{2}$). You cannot question $\underline{2}$, because $\underline{2}$ is the answer. I like this wisdom so much in meetings.

Evidence Wisdom answer

When the anointing is on you with the Holy spirit, God starts to use you to perform miracles like my spiritual father does, people of this world including your family (cousins, aunt and uncles) will start asking themselves questions about you and later they will sent people to spy on you, this happened to Jesus Christ of Nazareth. Read the below the scripture for more clarification;

Luke 7:20
"When the men were come unto him, they said, John Baptist hath sent us unto thee, saying, Art thou he that should come? Or look we for another..."

Look how Jesus cousin (John Baptist) treated Him (Jesus) yet God told him about the coming of the Messiah. Read below the wisdom of Jesus Christ answer;

Luke 7:22-23
"Then Jesus answering said unto them, Go your way, and tell John what things ye have seen and heard; how that the blind see, the lame walk, the lepers are cleansed, the deaf hear, the dead are raised, to the poor the gospel is preached. Luke7:23 And blessed is he, whosoever shall not be offended in me."

Sometimes it is important to respond with evidence to people testing you, because they are aware of you power and of whom you are. You need to take the dimension of demonstration ministry as a Christian with faith. Some people need touchable answers for them to see with their necked eye. You need to live evidence for people to understand you. Practice what you preach.

Notes:

Printed in the United States
by Baker & Taylor Publisher Services